Lessons

on

Life, Learning, and Leadership

for

Reading, Thinking About, and Discussing

About the Author

Brian Remer began his career as an educator and trainer by teaching English as a second language in Egypt. In an effort to make his teaching more interesting and effective he attended the SIT Graduate Institute where he discovered the power of experiential education. Since then he has been inventing and facilitating active learning strategies including the use of games, simulations, small group discussions, and short case studies. He is a recipient of the Ifill-Raynolds Lifetime Achievement award from the North American Simulation and Gaming Association. Brian realized that by reflecting upon personal experience, one could create significant learning from any situation. When a colleague suggested it was possible to write something meaningful in exactly 99 words, Brian took up the challenge. He wrote Say It Quick! which contains 99 stories, each exactly 99 words long, that inspire readers to learn significant lessons from every-day experiences.

For two years, Brian lived in Ecuador teaching English to business people through the Fulbright Commission while his wife led cross-cultural programs for U.S. students, and their daughter attended an all-Spanish school. The three of them enjoy international travel and hosting the friends they have met from other cultures. In his spare time, Brian keeps busy with swimming, cycling, reading science fiction, and transforming old books into secret treasure boxes. Currently he resides in rural Vermont where the winter, the scenic mountains, the people, and the culture of New England challenge him to continue learning every day.

Lessons

on

Life, Learning, and Leadership

for

Reading, Thinking About, and Discussing

Brian Remer

Pro Lingua Associates, Publishers
P.O. Box 1348
Brattleboro, Vermont 05302 USA
Office: 802-257-7779
Orders: 800-366- 4775
Email: info@ProLinguaAssociates.com
WebStore www.ProLinguaAssociates.com
SAN: 216-0579

At **Pro Lingua**
our objective is to foster an approach
to learning and teaching that we call
interplay, the **inter**action of language
learners and teachers with their materials,
with the language and culture,
and with each other in active, creative,
and productive **play**.

Lessons is based on *Say It Quick! 99-Word Stories About Leadership, Learning, and Life* which was written and copyrighted in 2011 by Brian Remer as a book of learning activities for business trainers and published by Workshops by Thiagi, Inc.

This book was designed and set by Arthur A. Burrows using the sans-serif typeface Candara, developed in 2005 for Microsoft by Gary Munch and published by Ascender. Sans-serif faces often appear to be stiff and mechanical, and though easy to read in short texts, they lack grace. This face, designed for digital reading, is said to be friendly, playful, and humanist. The letter shapes are open; the lines subtly flared. It is elegant when used for display or in small phrases, but comfortable to read in extended text.

The book was printed and bound by Royal Palm Press in Punto Gorda, Florida.
Printed in the United States of America

First printing 2014.

Contents

Learning ⌘ 17

Leadership ⌘ 33

Part Two

Acknowledgements

Thank you to all the relatives, friends, acquaintances, and unknown individuals who continue to provide inspiration for my learning every day and for Sivasailam "Thiagi" Thiagarajan who challenged me to write in as few words as possible.

On Third-Person Pronouns

In this book, Pro Lingua Associates is offering our solution to the vexing *he/she* problem. We have come to the conclusion that when a third-person singular pronoun is needed, and that person is indefinite (and hence gender is unknown or unimportant), we will use the third-person plural forms *they, them, their, theirs.* We are aware that historically these forms represent grammatical plurality. However, there are clear instances in the English language where the third-person plural form is used to refer to a preceding indefinite, grammatically singular pronoun. Examples:

Everyone says this, don't they.
Nobody agrees with us, but we will ignore them.

If you will accept the examples, it is not a major step to finding the following acceptable:

"The user of this book should find this easier because they can avoid the confusion and awkwardness of *he* or *she* or *he/she* and the implicit sexism of using *he* for everybody."

Long ago, English dispensed with *thee* and seems to be functioning quite well with two *yous.* So why not two *theys?*

Introduction

This *photocopyable* collection of "lessons" is intended for high-intermediate and advanced learners of English who are considering or are already involved in a higher education program. The "lessons" are presented as the author's observations of events and people in contemporary daily life, and his conclusions on the meaning and significance of his observations. Most of his observations focus on everyday aspects of contemporary American culture.

Part One of the book includes 92 observations, and **Part Two** includes the conclusions. The challenge to the learner is to read the brief observation, think about what can be learned from the observation, and then discuss their conclusions with classmates. Ultimately, after discussing the observation, the learners can then compare their conclusions with the author's in the second part of the book.

Essentially, the basic purpose of the book is to develop the skills of reading and thinking critically. This is not unlike reading a poem and then arriving at an interpretation of the poet's message or reading a fable or folk tale and discovering the moral.

In addition to addressing the skills of reading, reflective critical thinking, and discussion, the lessons offer an opportunity to develop the learner's vocabulary and gain additional insights into contemporary American culture.

In **Part Two**, in addition to the author's conclusions, there are brief cultural notes and potential lexical challenges for each lesson. These notes and challenges may be useful in preparing for the lesson and/or summarizing the entire activity.

The User's Guide on the next page describes a procedure for using the book.

User's Guide

Lessons can be used in a variety of ways, but a "standard" procedure is outlined below.

1. Photocopy a lesson (just the observation). They are printed two per page, and to prevent distraction, it is best to cut the page in half and give each learner only one of the lessons.

2. Have the learners look at and discuss the title of the lesson so that they will not begin the reading "cold." Very rarely is any reading activity done without some schema/context that provides a general expectation of the content of the reading.

3. (*optional*) If the reading has some cultural content that might be confusing or that might possibly obscure the point of the lesson, it may be best to explain this cultural feature. For example, in Lesson Life 4, it might be helpful to explain to the learners that every state has its own license plate – a metal tag on the back (sometimes also on the front) of a car with the state's name and often its motto (Live Free or Die) or nickname (Sunshine State).

4. (*optional*) Lexical items that could be troublesome are listed for each unit. (Most of them are beyond Pro Lingua's word frequency list at the 2400 level). It may be useful to put them on the board and work with them before asking the learners to read. These items can also be the basis for a post-lesson vocabulary session.

5. Have the learners read the passage. In most cases this should not take much more than one minute. Then check for comprehension. It my be best to ask pointed WH questions rather than saying "Do you have any questions?"

6. Have the learners individually try to come up with a conclusion – and write it down on their lesson.

7. Have the learners in groups (3 or 4 work well, although learners can also be paired) compare and discuss their conclusions, trying to arrive at a "best conclusion."

8. (*optional*) The groups can then compare and discuss their group conclusions.

9. Give the groups the author's conclusions and have them discuss the similarities with and differences from with their own.

10. (*optional*) Whenever it is appropriate, the learners can write their own lessons and conclusions. These can be used in class following the procedure above. The copyable form on page 77 can be used both to encourage this writing and to limit its length.

Life 1. Driving with Devon

Devon is a boy with autism. His biggest problem is that he reads and spells out every road sign on car trips. His parents dreaded driving with him. His annoying habit was a constant irritation – until they took a wrong turn onto a back street in Boston.

It was Devon who saved them by reciting every street they had driven through. Now Devon takes the copilot's seat for every road trip.

Life 2. The Need to Talk

I awoke excited, looking forward to the day's discoveries. But on the radio I heard distressing news. As it rolled around in my head, I sank deeper into the doldrums. By the time I arrived at the office my mood had become a mirror of that bleak, rainy November Monday.

Then I spoke to a colleague about the story I'd heard. He listened, nodding, silent. Immediately I felt better, less burdened. By noon, the sun had come out.

Life 3. Cultural Norms

After two years of driving in the congested, chaotic traffic of Ecuador, my wife adapted to the high-speed weaving and dodging that was an effective strategy abroad. Back in the U.S., behind the wheel, she found it difficult to change her habits.

Her driving had become downright dangerous – not to mention illegal!

Life 4. How Big Is Home?

While I was driving across New York on the interstate, a car approached me from behind. With lights flashing and horn blaring, a middle-aged couple smiled and waved enthusiastically as they sped past. "Hey, what's up," I thought. Then I noticed the license plate on their car: Nebraska, just like mine. I waved and smiled emphatically.

The three of us had yet to meet, but here, a thousand miles from home, we were neighbors, even friends. We could have exchanged gossip at a diner!

Life 5. Stay Inside the Lines

I bought a box of colored pencils for my daughter. Printed on the package was this endorsement: "Preferred by teachers." What, I wondered, does that really mean? Why do teachers like these pencils? Do they help children color inside the lines? Have schools "approved" these colors? There was no explanation.

Say, who cares what teachers think? Teachers don't use colored pencils; kids do. But parents buy them and *they* want to please teachers!

Life 6. The Passing Lane

Ahead of me climbing the steep mountain highway, three cars are following a very slow truck. Just ahead is a passing lane. The drivers all know this is the only passing lane for several miles. I can just imagine the tension in those cars as everyone tries to get around the lumbering truck before the passing lane ends. They are bumper to bumper at 60 mph!

Two cars pass the truck. Not me. But at the top of the hill, the truck makes a left turn onto another highway.

Life 7. Spreading the Word

My daughter and I were at an amusement park standing in line for the rollercoaster ride. We were hot, sweaty, and brain numb listening to the rollercoaster's theme song over and over. A few people began to leave. We became worried. Should we stay in line and get a return on our time investment? Should we leave and cut our losses?

"We'll be here for hours," my daughter loudly speculated. That was it. Instantly we were at the tail of a long line in the *opposite* direction as her words spread and people behind us began to leave.

Life 8. Enough Time

Some of Kate's college students complained that they didn't have adequate time to complete her assignments. Of course, some tasks cannot be done in the allotted time and some people need more time than others to accomplish the same thing. But Kate responded sternly, "There are 24 hours in every day. You had the same number of those hours as everyone else." Sound harsh?

Life 9. Being Present

Ken, a swimming buddy of mine, was a practicing Buddhist. He spent time in regular meditation and had traveled several times to Japan to deepen his awareness of "being in the moment." No doubt swimming was an extension of that contemplative practice.

One day he sauntered into the pool carrying his goggles and a strip of black cloth in one hand. When I saw him, I quietly asked, "Ken, is that your swim suit in your hand?" Embarrassed, he made a naked dash to the men's room!

Life 10. Instant Friendships

I was zooming down the highway on the way to an appointment. I'd borrowed my wife's car, a bright green VW Beetle. Coming toward me was the identical car. In the brief moment as we passed, I could see the passengers smiling and waving. We were friends in that instant! It seems we'll grab the slimmest thread of shared interest for beginning a relationship.

Now this never happens when I drive my old Subaru and meet another Subaru. We both bought the same car. Why did the bright green VW Beetle create an instant friendship?

Life 11. Always in Crisis

At a local social service agency, each case manager worked with up to ninety clients, solving problems and dealing with difficult situations on a daily basis. Their supervisors dashed from one disaster to the next while juggling meetings and paperwork. Everyone wore a cell phone. The most common comment was, "I'm in crisis!"

One summer, most everyone took a week off to attend a workshop out of town. During that time, not a single client phoned with an earth-shattering problem. Somehow they took care of themselves.

Life 12. Room to Wiggle

The steam room at the health club has just one switch: on or off. Flip the switch and wait. Is it really on? Something must be happening deep inside the plumbing guts of the health club, but you don't know what until a spray of steam shoots into the small room. That's when you know it's "on."

For machines and computers, a binary system is OK, but in real life there is wiggle room. A lot can happen between on and off, left and right, liberal and conservative.

Life 13. Reboot

At five on Friday, Joan's computer went on the fritz. The spreadsheet she was working on froze. The e-mail browser crashed. Her hand-held device wouldn't sync. The technical support team had already gone home. There was nothing else to do, so she pulled the plug and left for the weekend.

She returned on Monday anxious about re-entering a feedback loop of computer repair. But when the machine booted up, everything worked fine!

Life 14. Preoccupation

Once, when Diane was at the grocery store, she noticed a man in a wheelchair struggling to reach the items in the frozen food section. The door of the freezer and the height of the shelves made grasping things too difficult. She offered to help and retrieved several packages for him.

As she continued with her shopping, another customer stopped Diane with this observation, "I passed that fellow twice and never thought to ask if he needed help."

Life 15. A Public Statement

A white pickup truck, dented and beginning to rust, drove past. On the back was stenciled "Just Married 7/15/06." Yet this was more than a year after the nuptial date, and the sign had been made not with the usual shaving cream or cardboard sign but permanently!

I marveled that anyone would deliberately lower the resale value of even a modest vehicle. Was this simply an enthusiastic expression of lovesick newlyweds? Perhaps it was a perpetual reminder of what's really important. In either case, I wondered, "Would I do that?"

Life 16. The Trivial Things

One time I was reprimanded for leaving the meeting room at work in a mess. It was true I'd neglected to clean and put away a few things, but the criticism seemed a bit over the top. It bothered me all afternoon.

Later that day I was sweeping the deck at home. As I swept, I let the dirt, dust, and dead bugs drop through the spaces between the wooden floorboards. Usually "falling through the cracks" is not a good thing; it means someone got hurt, or left out. But here, letting things fall through the cracks was the best technique.

Life 17. Tired of Retirement

For years, Mitchell had a successful business selling shoes in our small town. He had a reputation for personable service and quality products. He thrived on the regular contact with all types of customers as well as business and community leaders.

At retirement, he moved with his wife to their northern Minnesota lake home, where Mitchell spent his days fishing and, literally, losing his mind. He became listless, irritable, forgetful. Dementia set in. When he took a part-time job selling cars, his usual alert, vibrant self returned immediately.

Life 18. Personal Issues

"Hi," I said to Molly as I rounded the corner of the building. Startled, she answered sheepishly, "Guess you caught me! I was trying to keep it a secret." I didn't know what she meant until I noticed the burning cigarette in her hand.

Newly hired, Molly was evidently trying to maintain appearances. She continued apologizing in spite of my reassurances. I suspect she wasn't as concerned that I knew about her habit as she was chagrined to be reminded of it.

Life 19. Competition's Curse

"You made me do that! I don't usually swim that fast," Gary said when we'd swum a few laps together. I hadn't known we were competing, so I was surprised at his remark, even though it was in jest.

Competition can be an inspiration to challenge oneself. But I'm interested in why Gary didn't claim his new speed for himself. He did all the swimming yet wouldn't give himself any credit. I wondered, can Gary get his new time again, or will he need a competitor for inspiration?

Life 20. Ignorance Is...

Our friend Laura took a job teaching in Spain and never left. She met a man in Pamplona, married, raised her children, and settled in as a member of his extended family. Her Spanish is fluent; she knows the local history and politics; she has visited every town in the surrounding area. She seems fully acculturated. Except she isn't.

"After 20 years, I still can't read the subtle social cues of class and status," Laura says, "And I don't want to! Brain surgeons, politicians, or fishermen, they're all just friends to me!"

Life 21. Passion and Purpose

Charles Schulz was clearly the parent and manager of a world of comic inspiration. He didn't just invent Charlie Brown; he created the whole universe of *Peanuts*. Daily comics, Sunday strips, books, TV, movies, products, endorsements, he was involved in all of it--including marketing the "empire." He even drew some cels for the animated flicks.

Before retiring, Schulz drew two months of comics. Astonishingly, he died the day before the last strip ran. The deep connection between passion and purpose was broken.

Life 22. All Dressed Up

My daughter, Tilden, had a terrific time at the sixth grade semi-formal dance – her first. And she learned a valuable lesson too.

"I spent three months finding the right dress and all day getting ready. I didn't have to do that," she explained. "I thought people would stand around and talk about who had the best dress, but we were too busy dancing. It was still fun to get dressed up, but I would have had just as much fun in jeans."

Life 23. Flowers and Weeds

When we built our home under a stand of maple trees, we were determined to keep the property as wooded as possible. Instead of planting a lawn, we seeded the area close to the house with wildflowers and perennials. The rest we left natural.

Wild blackberries sprang up quickly: whip-like strands with thorns like claws and bitter, tiny fruit. Fortunately, they were shaded out by a dense growth of ferns. But in the flower beds, those same ferns are crowding out the flowers we've planted.

Life 24. Confidence

With sweaty palms, I sat worrying in a side room. Interviewing for my first job after college, I had just met with a committee of twelve to answer their questions. Now I awaited the "verdict." Would they give me the job? And worse, if I got it, could I do it? I wasn't sure!

Then I relaxed: If they could determine from a resume and an interview that I was the right person, then I, who knew myself so much better, could probably pull it off.

Oh, yes, I got the job!

Life 25. Imagine!

Jeff was not fond of the city but he lived in an apartment above a busy Manhattan street. The rush of urban living – especially the noise of traffic – began to affect his sense of well-being. So, when a friend suggested he spend his vacation on the island of Martha's Vineyard, Jeff did not hesitate.

Two weeks surrounded by gulls and waves healed Jeff's spirit with lasting impact. He felt great! Back in New York, he still awoke with the sound of "surf" in his ears – even though it was really the traffic far below his window!

Life 26. Your Center

Fronton, a game like handball played on a two-walled court, originated in the Basque Country. You can find a fronton court in every Basque village no matter how small. It's usually at the central square and may even share a wall with an ancient church. Across the square you'll see a small bar or a restaurant.

It's hardly a surprise to find a fronton court, church, and bar side by side. What does that say about Basque culture? Play, spirit, and friendship are foremost.

Life 27. Writer's Block

Kate was stuck in her writing and stuck in the snow. Her words fell like slush on her paper, and the wet, heavy snow outside made her back ache. But the snow had to be shoveled. Grumbling under her breath, she dug into the snow again.

Then she noticed the gently drifting snowflakes and crisp, silent air. She took a deep breath of winter, chose to be present in the moment, and felt her body relax.

With the rhythm of physical work, she entered a state of flow, finishing quickly – and gained new ideas for her writing in the process!

Life 28. Focus of Attention

With neon signs that take up the side of a whole building, vendors and musicians on every corner, traffic racing through the streets, and faces from seven continents, Times Square was a night of entertainment all by itself. I was captivated. But trying to find the restaurant where my friend was waiting, I walked right past it – twice!

I was focused on what was happening across the street, and ignored the details on my side of the street.

Life 29. Wants and Needs

At the annual St. Patrick's Day breakfast of the Holyoke Chamber of Commerce, the tables were decorated in green and silver. Each place had a gift-wrapped candle for the guest. After the mayor's speech and announcement of the parade queen, it came time to leave. On the way out, I snatched an extra green candle "for a friend."

Wait. Why was I doing this? I don't need candles. I'm not even Irish!

Life 30. Perspective

I love travel. Every day is an adventure with multiple small reminders that you are a foreigner. And the bonus: re-entry is an adventure too. With enough time away, everything looks different upon your return. You ask, "Why do we do things this particular way, and do we have to?" Imagine! The highway signs are green here instead of blue as in Europe!

How can I keep that foreigner's inquisitiveness alive? So quickly the novel becomes the norm. By the time I arrive home from the airport, those green signs don't look so odd.

Life 31. Threats

A Vermont town meeting is not representative. Anyone can attend and speak – and most everyone does. Last year we spent 45 minutes debating a $3000 increase in the town budget to contract for the local ambulance service. That came to an increase in taxes of only $1.50 per household. Why was the debate so furiously hot? Because the service said they wouldn't work in the town unless their proposed increase was voted in.

People felt threatened and nearly voted it down. The ambulance service learned that you'll be dead on arrival if you drive the wrong vehicle to town meeting!

Life 32. Doing the Dishes

I don't mind washing the dishes. It's a way to help out when I haven't assisted with the cooking. There's one thing I've never been able to get a handle on, though. Just as I dry my hands, I'll turn around and find another dirty plate, cup, or pot hiding in a corner. How did I miss that? Can I ever get all the dishes clean?

Then I realized that this is what dishes are for. They are supposed to get dirty, be washed, and get dirty again.

Learning 1. Turn Right to Go Left

Busy intersections are few in my hometown, but during tourist season you can wait a long time to make a left turn onto a crowded highway. Recently I just could not find a break in the traffic flowing east that coincided with one in the traffic flowing west.

Then an idea! Switching signals, I turned right into the flow. Less than a tenth of a mile later, I turned left into a parking lot and took another right, joining the traffic in the direction of my original intent.

Learning 2. Wasting Work Time

Listening to the radio, I heard that Americans waste an average of two hours at work every day. That translates into $759 billion lost!

Me? I never "waste" time at work. A walk to the coffee pot puts me in touch with other people, their projects, their problems, and their needs. I'm busy making connections, building social capital. Even the physical act of moving gets my brain working in different ways, exploring new paths. I always return to my desk with several new ideas.

Learning 3. Looking and Finding

Paul was a bird watcher. He especially loved raptors, and had sighted hundreds of hawks – all kinds – over the years. But he had never seen owls in the wild. Not surprising, since they are silent, stealthy, and nocturnal! Then one day, driving across the state, he spotted an owl and slowed to catch the details.

It was amazing that he noticed an owl in broad daylight. Even more amazing, though, was that he sighted four more that same day!

Learning 4. Limits

Three times a week is my swimming goal. The results are better health physically, mentally, and emotionally. But that doesn't mean that I am always motivated. Some days, looking at the end of the pool 75 feet away, I feel tired before I begin. Too much work!

A dip in Sweet Pond is different. When I look down its length, I see a half mile of glassy smooth water that feels like satin as I dive in. I could swim forever here, relaxed but challenged!

Learning 5. Teaching a Lesson

Carol confessed that she didn't like to cook. She recalled her
Home Economics class. She was beating an egg with a fork. The
teacher said, "Not so much noise. I don't want to hear any clicking
when you're beating those eggs!" Now, half a lifetime later, Carol
admitted, "That only made me want to do it more. And I always
think of that woman whenever I beat eggs!"

How would that teacher react if she knew the only thing Carol
remembers from her class is having been scolded?

Learning 6. Too Much Talk!

I was having a heart-to-heart conversation with my daughter. She
was about to enter her teen years, and I knew she would benefit
from my reflections of how to survive those troubling pubescent
times. As I revved up for a helpful review of my main points, I looked
over in her direction.

She was staring into the middle distance with glazed eyes and
slouched shoulders. She'd been turned off. I'd been tuned out.

Learning 7. Who Knew?

At three and a half, my daughter was a pacifier junkie. She only popped it in her mouth after daycare, yet no amount of encouragement could induce her to kick the habit.

One day, my wife and I were discussing a report that the chemical softener in pacifiers could be carcinogenic. Our daughter interrupted to ask what we were talking about. We explained, in simple terms, that her pacifier might be dangerous for her long-term health. Without a word, she took it out of her mouth. Cold turkey.

Learning 8. The Wrong Notes

When Travis, the only saxophone player in the school's fifth grade band, began his concert solo by playing "Hot Cross Buns" instead of "Merrily We Roll Along," he stopped, waved his arm, and said, "No, wait! That's not it. Wrong one. This is it." To everyone's relief, he then led the band in a spirited rendition of the correct number.

The pursuit of excellence, our preoccupation with perfection, doesn't leave much room for mistakes – even when someone is learning a complicated task.

Learning 9. 100,000 Teachers

When we lived in Ecuador for two years, one of my personal goals was to learn Spanish. So I was upset when Giovanni, my tutor, announced that he would be leaving the country to take another job. Learning a second language was traumatic for me, and Giovanni was terrific at tailoring lessons to my particular interests and needs. How could I ever hope to find a replacement?

Then, while riding a crowded Quito bus, I found the solution. Everyone spoke Spanish. I was surrounded by thousands of teachers!

Learning 10. Overdue and Unprepared

One Saturday I noticed that my car was 10 days overdue for its annual safety inspection, so I drove around in search of an auto mechanic. I finally found a shop that was open and scheduled an appointment for that afternoon. I returned for the fifteen-minute inspection only to realize I was missing the insurance papers – an essential element of the process!

Rats! A whole Saturday wasted and nothing to show for it – except I've got a story to tell. And that's good enough to keep me on my toes for a while!

Learning 11. On Mobility

At a small church in rural Vermont, everything is attached to wheels. The cabinets, bookcases, tables, chairs, and room dividers for the Sunday classrooms are all on rollers. When it's time for a special event such as the strawberry supper or Christmas bazaar, everything but the kitchen sink is wheeled away, leaving one large space for the event. A few years ago, the whole church was lifted off its foundation and rolled 700 feet away to accommodate a road expansion project.

Learning 12. On a Roll

In the office kitchen, a roll of paper towels sits on the counter. Though handy, it takes up space, is hard to dispense, and often ends up in the sink. I did nothing about it. Then one day I found the paper towels hanging above the counter on a towel holder.

128 sheets per roll and a minimum of one roll a week for seven years; that's at least 46,592 sheets. How many squares of paper were used before somebody fixed this nuisance?

Learning 13. A Crumby Day

A casual "Hello" to Carol got me an earful! The day was still new but she was already out of sorts. "I hope it gets better, because it's lousy so far!" She explained that her husband had left crumbs all over the stove simply because they were part of a mess he hadn't made. "I don't need another irresponsible child in the house," she declared. She let a few crumbs spoil her whole day.

Learning 14. A Perfect Smile

At my last dental appointment, I got more than the usual fluoride treatment. I learned about smiles. My dentist explained that we decide whether someone's smile is "normal," whether it looks right, by noticing the blank spaces. Teeth are important, but we get our sense of symmetry from the empty space around them – without even realizing it!

Similarly, we judge people based upon what isn't there: the intent behind their actions, the tone underlying their words, the assumptions about their ethnicity.

Learning 15. A Father's Choice

I'm surprised and delighted that at age 14, my daughter still asks me to help pick out her clothes. Naturally, I choose something conservative: a long sleeve top and loose-fitting jeans. Her choice has flair: a top with skinny shoulder straps and a short, swishy skirt. That's what she wore. Does it matter that my suggestion was rejected? In the end, she looks great.

But why did she bother asking anyway? What about my suggestion? Was it merely to see what not to do in the teenage world?

Learning 16. Sugar Coating

At the grocery superstore with its polished aisles and fully stocked shelves, you can find delicious-looking cinnamon rolls made right there. They smell like grandma's and they're slathered with a thick layer of frosting. But the bread-like substance underneath resembles a woolen mitten. Unfortunately, the baker uses so much sugar above, you might not realize the inside is second class.

I wish I could remember that! And, if I'm going to spend money to store the calories around my middle, I might at least get something that tastes first rate!

Learning 17. Less is More

I had traveled across the country to attend a three-day workshop by a famed facilitator, so I was especially disappointed when his opening presentation about interactive learning strategies was interrupted by a blaring electronic alarm. "Break time!" he announced.

Weird, I thought, he never even stated his main point. I turned to another participant and began a discussion about the definition of interactivity.

After a few minutes, the facilitator remarked, "Hey, nobody took a break! You're all still going at it. Seems the less I talk, the more you learn."

Learning 18. In Sight

"Without my glasses I didn't recognize you until I heard the rhythm of your swimming," Sissy admitted at the pool.

If I lost my glasses, I'd have to make big changes. I'd have to listen more, rely upon other senses, slow down. I'd need to develop alternative resources, invent coping strategies. Perhaps I'd become more thoughtful, more reflective. Mostly, I hope I would concentrate on building and reinforcing relationships with the people I truly care about.

Learning 19. Deliver the Message

"Children are the living messages we send to a time we will not see."

I first encountered this quote by John W. Whitehead on the stationery of a local childcare organization. Whitehead is a noted civil rights lawyer concerned with defending the most vulnerable of our society. His statement highlights the importance of parenting, teaching, and being a good community member.

It makes me think: If a picture is worth a thousand words, how many million words is a child worth? In fact, we adults were all children once, weren't we?

Learning 20. First Amendment

Bumper stickers are a popular medium for sharing ideas: free speech and self-expression. People state their passions and reveal bits of their personality, politics, and sense of humor. Whether clever, contemplative, or caustic, they invite tailgating for curiosity's sake.

But I can't help wondering. What does a yellow ribbon mean for her, exactly? What does a peace symbol signify for him? Like a TV commercial or a politician's sound bite, the catchy phrases accelerate and disappear before one can formulate a follow-up question.

Learning 21. An Empty Desk

For two years I shared an office with Mary Ellen, a high-energy multi-tasker. I always knew when she was under a deadline for a big project or grant because she would spend at least half a day clearing off her desk. Rearranging, filing, stacking, dusting, was she wasting time? Cleaning a space to work? Clearing her mind? I couldn't tell, but her projects got done on time and her grants were funded. She was very successful!

Learning 22. Mud Season

One muddy spring day I loaded the garbage into the car for a trip to the dumpster at the bottom of the hill. I inched carefully down our unpaved road, trying to avoid the deep sloppy tracks other people had made by riding the high ground. No use! The muck grabbed the tires and I could only hang on and keep moving. The car steered itself, scraping bottom all the way.

Reaching the pavement I congratulated myself and sped off. How glad I was to be out of a rut! But I wasn't really. The garbage was still in the car!

Learning 23. Dead and Alive

On a springtime walk in the woods I came upon an unusual sight. Where a grove of sugar maples had stood last summer, now there were only stumps. Though disappointed, I was curious to see that each stump was soaking wet and surrounded by a puddle of water even though it had not been raining.

Looking closer, I realized that this wasn't water. It was sap, the raw material of maple syrup! Loggers thought the tree was dead but the roots thought it was alive.

Learning 24. High Expectations

Surrounded by friends and food in a small fishing village near Bilbao, I thought this would be a perfect opportunity to improve my Spanish. But forget about speaking. I couldn't even decipher the topic of conversation! I was completely frustrated.

Then I realized: we were nine people at the table and eight were speaking simultaneously! Not to mention the three children and a loud TV in the next room. Even a native speaker couldn't keep up with all that talk. I began to relax.

Learning 25. Ask Stupid Questions

"Why is the light switch in the hall outside and not in the bathroom itself?" Amused by the "obvious" simplicity of the query, our Basque friend replied, "To avoid electric shocks, of course!"

This is the beauty of cultural exchange. We get used to asking stupid questions, and sometimes, when new to a subject, we are too ignorant to know what questions to ask. Back in our own culture, we sometimes know too much to consider asking questions and then regret that we didn't.

Learning 26. Try Again

Under the big circus tent, it was the tightrope walker's most spectacular stunt: a double back flip to land on the rope. Add to the suspense that this was not the typical jaded road show. This was Circus Smirkus, a troupe of teenagers with all the talent of an adult professional team.

Two attempts ended with legs and wire entangled. But by the third try he landed on his feet and the crowd erupted in applause – louder than if he'd succeeded the first time!

Learning 27. Potential

Bob was a writer who wanted to quit journalism. He applied to many organizations as a grant writer. Though he had several interviews, an offer never materialized. One day, a would-be employer called, not with a job but with a suggestion: "You've got too much talent to be a grant writer," she said. "You're executive director material."

Since then, Bob has successfully led several organizations because a stranger's comment changed his self-concept.

Learning 28. Oops?

The car kept moving, so I couldn't ask the driver what her license plate meant. It said, "NOMSTKS." It must mean "No Mistakes." Now I'm really curious. Why would someone want to be error free? Mistakes cause problems but they also produce powerful learning. The only big mistakes of life are the ones we don't learn from!

Maybe it means the driver has no regrets, no remorse. She will bulldoze anyone as she speeds through life.

Too bad for the spelling error and missing vowels. Perhaps it really means "No Mystics."

Learning 29. Real Lessons

For three years I taught English in Egypt. Once a week, I volunteered to tutor a group of disadvantaged teens. But that had been 10 years ago and now I was back for a visit, touring a new school.

Entering the computer classroom, the professor introduced himself. "I'm Emad, one of the kids you tutored. You know, I didn't learn any English from you." I was crushed, until he added, "But I did learn how to be a good teacher!" I never realized I'd given that lesson!

Learning 30. Missed Messages

Waiting to board my flight at gate B7, I hear, for the third time, an important safety message blaring over the PA system. "Liquids and hazardous materials are not allowed beyond the security checkpoint."

Now, everyone listening to this message has already cleared security and been stripped of offending liquids! If no one has found illegal items by now, I doubt they ever will. Yet the announcement has drowned out other useful information about flight and gate changes.

Learning 31. The Slow Learner

One sweltering summer day, I sought relief on the screened porch. An enormous housefly was bouncing against the screen, trying to get out. Feeling charitable, I waited until it got to the door, then swung it open. But the fly kept bashing into the screen door anyway. I pushed the door open further. Still the fly bouncd off the screen, never knowing a right angle turn would set it free. Finally I let the door swing shut.

Learning 32. Happiness

Mary has had a hard life. The oldest of six children, she was always a caretaker. But when her parents fell ill, Mary became the "teenaged manager" of the whole family helping her siblings survive emotional and financial hardships. As an adult, she works and lives with people who have severe mental and physical disabilities. You'd think she'd be pessimistic yet she is one of the happiest people I know. How?

"With life in constant chaos," she says, "I realized that the only thing I could control was my own attitude."

Leadership 1. Creating Change

I just experienced a sudden pang of hunger! Searching the house for a quick fix, I find a bag of corn chips and grab a fistful. Munching away, I immediately feel better. The food has yet to hit my stomach but already the hunger is diminishing. Interesting!

So often I worry about making change happen and spend time anxiously waiting for the final result. Sometimes doing anything, just creating movement toward the goal, is enough to get relief, to see progress.

Leadership 2. What's Your Contribution?

Bob hated meetings. You could witness it in his tone of voice, his body language, his demeanor, and his droll, sarcastic comments. He was famous for his opinion about meetings. Yet as head of his department, attending and leading meetings was a big part of his responsibility.

Surprisingly, Bob taught me the secret to having a great meeting. He would often leave a meeting grumbling that he hadn't gotten anything out of it. But I noticed that he hadn't put anything into the meeting either!

Leadership 3. Empowerment

Linda was a great boss. More like a coach than a supervisor, she helped me strive for my potential and offered me opportunities to learn and grow professionally and personally. Acutely aware of power differences, she didn't discriminate between me and her office assistant, Isabel.

One day, Isabel confided, "Linda's always trying to get me to go to these fancy retreats but I just want to stay here and type."

Leadership 4. Taking a Stand on Meetings

In some organizations, no one is allowed to sit during meetings. The idea is that if we have to stand, we'll finish the meeting and get back to business. Problem is, this assumes a limited use for meetings: giving orders or reporting. Both could be accomplished as easily in an email!

If the meeting is to analyze, create, learn, solve, or celebrate, then make a place for conversation. Spread the table with linens, flowers, coffee, and snacks and have a meaningful conversation.

Leadership 5. Climbing Toward Goals

Mt. Monadnock is located in southwest New Hampshire. At 3165 ft. it is the most frequently climbed mountain in North America! Fitness hikers, older folks, and families are among its 125,000 annual visitors. At the top, hikers enjoy a panoramic view of all six New England states.

Monadnock has one summit, one goal, for all those people, yet there are five trails to reach it. What's important to you: vistas, wildflowers, history, solitude? Choose a path but get to the top!

Leadership 6. The Best Holiday

'Twas the day after Christmas. A vacation for me but not, unfortunately, for the rest of my family, so I'm left to my own devices. What to do? Let's see: there's that picture that needs to be hung, but I'll have to paint over the black marks left by the photo of Aunt Mable.

Wow. There are black marks in every room. Two hours later I'm still spot painting the house. Stranger still, I'm enjoying it. What's going on? Oh, yes. Painting was my choice.

Leadership 7. Seeing the Big Picture

I needed to find my way through a large, unfamiliar metro area. Fortunately I was able to borrow my sister's car equipped with a GPS navigation system. With this handy device I drove through city traffic during rush hour with ease. I just kept one eye on the readout and listened for the prompts.

But the trip wasn't without anxiety. Several times, the gentle metallic voice gave instructions that were counterintuitive. At 65 mph it was very disconcerting!

Leadership 8. Hot? Cold?

How's the water today? That's a common question among the morning lap swimmers at the pool. On any given day, one person will say it's too hot while another complains that it's too cold. There is no pleasing everyone!

What I find most difficult, though, is not having either hot or cold water but having both. The biggest stressor is experiencing the sudden shock of going from hot to cold as you swim a lap. It's nearly impossible to become acclimated.

Leadership 9. Choose Chaos

When my daughter was a young reader she asked, "Have you noticed how the word 'chaos' looks a lot like the word 'choice'?" Though you may not agree, the two actually have a strong relationship.

Scientists describe chaos as a state in which all potentialities are present within a given boundary. Anything is possible. Randomness rules. The outcome is unpredictable and uncertain – until a choice is made and one future path becomes more certain than the others.

Leadership 10. Who's to Blame?

My friend Jean informed me that 25% of the pollution in California actually comes from China. The culprit? Coal-fired power plants. The Chinese plan to build more than 500 new coal power plants in the next 10 years!

It's something of a relief to discover that we aren't responsible for all the pollution in California, that it isn't all our fault. In New England we often have to contend with the pollution from power plants in the Midwest. And I imagine that the pollution in Eastern Europe goes to... Asia?

Leadership 11. Being the Crowd

When I walked into the pool for a swim, a small group was just leaving. I overheard them grumbling about how crowded the pool was that day. When I mentioned this to Phil, a swimming buddy, he replied with irony, "They would certainly know about crowds. They brought one with them!"

He was right. When you add four people to this small place, it's suddenly very crowded, but the place was nearly empty now.

Leadership 12. Trash or Treasure

"Used bicycle parts – Some junk"

That's the label on a typical cardboard box in Ralph's garage. This barn beside his home where he has lived (and accumulated) for over 50 years used to have space for three cars. Today there is barely room for one. The building is stuffed with treasures only Ralph would value. Bent yard tools, charred clothes from a house fire, a child's kindergarten craft projects, boxed and labeled, fill the space from floor to ceiling. He can find anything.

Leadership 13. Built to Last

The Incan ruins of Peru's Machu Picchu are famous for their massive stone walls fitted together without mortar. Even after hundreds of years, the blocks are so tight, there's not the slightest gap between them. What's more, each block has a unique, irregular shape. Some are larger than an SUV!

Why build with such irregular stones when clearly any shape could have been fashioned?

Because these walls have withstood earthquakes when walls of standardized block have crumbled. How might this apply to management?

Leadership 14. Open for Business?

Savoring early morning coffee and the ocean view from my booth in Breakers Restaurant at the Ashworth Hotel, I was startled by a loud tapping on the front door. Someone wanted to get in for breakfast. Looking around the deserted restaurant, I called for the cook to open the door.

Here it was 30 minutes after "opening" and the front door was still locked. You'd think someone would have checked – especially since they'd had to unlock the side door from the hotel for me earlier!

Leadership 15. The Accidental Leader

Through the corridor, down the stairs, around the corner, and into the copy room, all the way I was just a few paces behind Nancy. The coincidental similarity of our travels through the office caused her to tease, "Are you following me?"

"No," I quipped. "Are you leading me?" We laughed together, but it made me think. If people have the same goal and objectives, there is really very little difference between leading and following.

Leadership 16. Motion Sickness

During my parents' first visit to Vermont, they drove along Route 100 for a scenic tour of fall foliage through the Green Mountains. When asked how they liked it, Dad waxed poetic about the bright colors and picturesque New England villages. He loved the challenge of navigating the curved, rolling highways.

But Mom, accustomed to the flat, straight roads of South Dakota, could only remember the green tinge to her own complexion as she tried to calm her rolling stomach!

Leadership 17. Simply Exact

My friend Sarah likes to be precise. Send her a simple email, and she'll reply with an essay. She wants to be clear, exact, understood. But, when given so many details, you begin to wonder about things that hadn't occurred to you.

You write to Sarah for clarification. She replies with more specifics, leaving you curious about a few instances she hasn't outlined. After another round of messages, you find yourself questioning the meaning and looking for hidden implications. Sarah's "clarity" becomes a fog of confusion. Her main point has been obscured.

Leadership 18. Great Groups

Andy is a wonderful musician, teacher, and storyteller. He teaches in schools, calls at square dances, leads choral groups, and plays a mean accordion. What Andy doesn't realize is that he's an expert at fostering teamwork. He has the ability to lead without being in charge – even though he's the "director."

One comment he made while leading a choir of novice singers summarizes his philosophy. He said, "Here's how you harmonize. Listen to the person next to you and sing something a little different." All share one objective, but each contributes uniquely.

Leadership 19. Turning and Changing

I ran for miles and miles beside my daughter as she learned to ride a bicycle. I was determined she would learn without ever falling down. For weeks we practiced.

Balancing her was awkward, especially when she turned away from me. But when she turned to my direction, I could support her as she leaned into the turn. And the harder she leaned, the tighter and faster the turn. So, turning a bicycle is like falling!

Leadership 20. Motivation That's Habit Forming

Everyone knows it's tough to quit smoking, but why do people start? Cigarettes have a warning label. In Europe it covers half the pack! What's the motivation to begin an activity that everyone knows will eventually kill them? No one would drink a household cleaner even though the warning label is less prominent!

Despite the obvious dangers, many people begin smoking to be cool, to be in, to be part of the group. Social belonging is one of the strongest human needs – and it crosses cultures.

Leadership 21. Making Changes

At a statewide leadership training course I facilitated, everyone returned to their same chair after lunch. I mentioned that this was an opportunity to learn from other leaders and asked people to sit at a table with all new participants. I let them, as leaders themselves, figure out how to make the change.

In the ensuing chaos, the leaders "conspired." Some moved with a buddy. Others brought along familiar "comfort" items. One whole table stayed intact, hoping I wouldn't notice!

Leadership 22. No, Gracias

A txoco is a Basque club where thirty or more friends cook and feast for up to six hours. The food just keeps coming. After only the second course, my belt was ready to burst. "Leave something on your plate so people don't try to keep filling it," my wife advised.

Sounds like the office: pretend to be busy so the boss doesn't pile more onto your plate! A clean plate could also mean you're evaluating your latest efforts, getting ready for a new project, resting, digesting.

Leadership 23. All Together

Imagine dining out with a group of lifelong friends – a big group – twenty-four in all! After five hours of food and highly spirited conversation up and down the long table, the woman across from you bursts into boisterous song. Shortly, the whole table is singing loud enough to rattle the windows.

This is a common experience in parts of Spain but, as a foreigner, I was worried about disturbing other restaurant patrons. Then, to my surprise, all the other diners joined in! People on the street heard us and added their voices too.

Leadership 24. Change Recipe

At cousin Donna's Thanksgiving dinner the butter is homemade. Here's the recipe: fill a jelly jar three quarters with cream, then shake, jiggle, vibrate, wobble, agitate. Keep the jar moving. Repeat. Repeat again. By now, your arms are tired, nothing has happened, and you are ready to give up. Many people do.

But with persistence, a moment comes when you feel a "thunk" and a lump of fresh butter magically replaces the liquid in your jar. Just like that!

Leadership 25. Lead Me, Please!

It's obvious the regulars of the Senior Aerobics Club come to socialize as much as to exercise. Jean was chatting with a friend as they waited for the instructor to arrive one early morning. "I don't know why we need a leader. We all know the routine," she said. "I guess it's just easier." Her friend agreed.

When the regular teacher never arrived, they suffered with a substitute, someone known as "that bossy woman from New York."

Leadership 26. Second Life

An aluminum pot with a hole, paper shopping bags 10 years old (one has a dated receipt inside), a tattered dish towel – these are the items in use at Dwight's house. It isn't that Dwight can't afford a new pot or that he doesn't notice that his towels are threadbare. As he says, "I don't like to throw things away."

Dwight could be dismissed as a hopeless eccentric, but I like the hidden message: his undying hope (no, an expectation!). Things can always be made useful.

Leadership 27. Pressing Matters

Yes, I should have done it the night before, but this morning I was madly trying to iron my shirt. Now I would be late for the meeting. The meeting! I'd spent days planning, clearing the agenda, sending reminders, ordering refreshments. The outcome was critical. Had I really checked all the details, factored all the political angles, considered the long-range implications?

Finally, the shirt's done. The front looks sharp. But what's this? I've pressed a huge, permanent crease into the back!

Leadership 28. Itching to Succeed

I've been driven mad with the prickling under my collar, like tiny, sharp-clawed insects, after a haircut. Ready to scream, I immediately jump into a hot shower!

But at my last barber visit, I wore a white T-shirt. When the smock was removed, the fine dusting of dark shavings was obvious. The barber grabbed a horsehair brush and gave my clothing several extra whisks to do away with all the clippings. Immediate relief!

Leadership 29. Management Training

To juggle three scarves, hold two in your right hand and one in your left. Toss one scarf from the right then one from the left. As your left arm descends, snatch the first scarf out of the air. With your right, throw the third scarf and catch the second on the way down. Alternate your throwing hands, using each hand to catch as it drops back from a throw.

The tricky part: if you watch the scarf you just threw, you won't be ready to catch the next.

Leadership 30. Better Decisions

Coffee cake, cookies, fruit salad; there was everything short of a full breakfast at the all-staff meeting. I'd planned to take only a muffin; I'd just eaten, after all. But the poor thing looked lonely on my clean, white plate, so I added more food until the plate was loaded down.

I wasn't that hungry, but it's easy to forget that, whatever space we have, we tend to fill – whether we need to or not. Maybe I should have taken a smaller plate.

Life Conclusions

Life 1. Driving with Devon ⌘ page 1
Sometimes in a different situation a person's deficit becomes an asset.

Life 2. The Need to Talk ⌘ page 1
Saying something out loud, getting it off your chest and onto the table, can change your mood. It only takes a few words to clear the air.

Life 3. Cultural Norms ⌘ page 2
With enough exposure, nearly any behavior becomes "normal"; but change the circumstances, and it can become abnormal in no time.

Life 4. How Big Is Home? ⌘ page 2
The farther you are from home, the bigger home becomes.

Life 5. Stay Inside the Lines ⌘ page 3
It's easy to please the wrong person if you haven't thought about why you're trying to please them in the first place.

Life 6. The Passing Lane ⌘ page 3
Some problems take care of themselves.

Life 7. Spreading the Word ⌘ page 4
Our words (and our reputation) can spread faster than our actions!

Life 8. Enough Time ⌘ page 4
Usually when we "don't have time" it's because we choose to do something else. Isn't it really about priorities?

Life 9. Being Present ⌘ page 5
Even someone "in the moment" can benefit from a gentle reminder to be less preoccupied.

Life 10. Instant Friendships ⌘ page 5
People want to discover something in common, but the more uncommon, the better.

Life 11. Always in Crisis ⌘ page 6
   Who really creates all the emergencies?

Life 12. Room to Wiggle ⌘ page 6
   How often do we needlessly confine ourselves to only two options?

Life 13. Reboot ⌘ page 7
   When you've tried everything, the best solution may be to leave things alone. The trick: knowing when to act quickly and when to walk away.

Life 14. Preoccupation ⌘ page 7
   It's easy to be preoccupied with our own "shopping list" and be oblivious to the needs of others.

Life 15. A Public Statement ⌘ page 8
   Which of our commitments are we willing to express openly and permanently?

Life 16. The Trivial Things ⌘ page 8
   It helps to know what's important and when to sweep the insignificant things out of our lives and relationships.

Life 17. Tired of Retirement ⌘ page 9
   If you've got a purpose, you've got life.

Life 18. Personal Issues ⌘ page 9
   What we are least proud of may be what we are most desperate to hide.

Life 19. Competition's Curse ⌘ page 10
   A focus on competition can prevent us from establishing our own standards.

Life 20. Ignorance Is... ⌘ page 10
   Sometimes ignorance is a benefit!

Life 21. Passion and Purpose ⌘ page 11
   Cut links to a meaningful life, and you may lose your reason for living.

Learning Conclusions

Learning 1. Turn Right to Go Left ⌘ page 17
Sometimes the indirect approach is better.

Learning 2. Wasting Work Time ⌘ page 17
Perhaps we ought to redefine "waste" and "work" and how we value them.

Learning 3. Looking and Finding ⌘ page 18
When you are clear about what you are looking for, you begin to find it everywhere.

Learning 4. Limits ⌘ page 18
How easily we allow ourselves to be affected by how far we see.

Learning 5. Teaching a Lesson ⌘ page 19
Often, the littlest comments have the biggest impact!

Learning 6. Too Much Talk! ⌘ page 19
Too much of a good thing had become just another lecture. Less is more.

Learning 7. Who Knew? ⌘ page 20
We never really know how much a person comprehends!

Learning 8. The Wrong Notes ⌘ page 20
Bravo to the "performer" who can make a mistake and confidently move on.

Learning 9. 100,000 Teachers ⌘ page 21
An expert is not always better than everyday expertise.

Learning 10. Overdue and Unprepared ⌘ page 21
There's always something to be learned from mistakes.

Learning 11. On Mobility ⌘ page 22

Whatever your belief system, make it strong but not static. Be ready to move and change when you have to.

Learning 12. On a Roll ⌘ page 22

Sometimes we tolerate something that was inefficient and unhelpful just because that's the way it is!

Learning 13. A Crumby Day ⌘ page 23

A little problem may really be a metaphor for a much bigger issue.

Learning 14. A Perfect Smile ⌘ page 23

Like reading between the lines, the space between has a bigger impact than what's obvious.

Learning 15. A Father's Choice ⌘ page 24

Even the ideas that aren't used can contribute to success.

Learning 16. Sugar Coating ⌘ page 24

Rather than going for the "sugar coating," focus on quality to begin with.

Learning 17. Less is More ⌘ page 25

Interactive learning elegantly demonstrated!

Learning 18. In Sight ⌘ page 25

Sometimes losing something you think you need (even if only in your mind's eye) helps you focus on what's really important.

Learning 19. Deliver the Message ⌘ page 26

Aren't we each delivering a million-word living message right now?

Learning 20. First Amendment ⌘ page 26

Bumper stickers, commercials, and sound bites allow us to be superficial and play hit and run with important social issues.

Learning 21. An Empty Desk ⌘ page 27

Call it procrastination if you like, but preparation for the activity is as important for success as the activity itself.

Leadership Conclusions

Leadership 1. Creating Change ⌘ page 33
We don't need to do big things to create change If we just start moving.

Leadership 2. What's Your Contribution? ⌘ page 33
If you want a great meeting, plan to make a contribution!

Leadership 3. Empowerment ⌘ page 34
You can offer to empower people, but they have to be ready and want to make changes for themselves.

Leadership 4. Taking a Stand on Meetings ⌘ page 34
Shape the environment to your needs. Don't force people into the shape you need.

Leadership 5. Climbing Toward Goals ⌘ page 35
If we agree on our goal, our values will help us decide the right path.

Leadership 6. The Best Holiday ⌘ page 35
When we follow our own decisions, we are motivated and satisfied.

Leadership 7. Seeing the Big Picture ⌘ page 36
Discrete instructions do not always make sense if you don't know the whole picture.

Leadership 8. Hot? Cold? ⌘ page 36
Whether in team responsibilities, household rules, or tax laws, it's the inconsistencies that produce the most discontent.

Leadership 9. Choose Chaos ⌘ page 37
When we are surrounded by chaos, we are also surrounded by maximum possibility, by choices. Get unstuck. Choose and move.

Leadership 10. Who's to Blame? ⌘ page 37
We all live upwind from someone else! No country is an island.

Leadership 21. Making Changes ⌘ page 43

Thus, a simple request became a lesson in overcoming the barriers to change.

Leadership 22. No, Gracias ⌘ page 43

Clean plates may not be empty.

Leadership 23. All Together ⌘ page 44

Collaboration can be contagious!

Leadership 24. Change Recipe ⌘ page 44

To produce change, stick to it. What seems like ineffective agitation can suddenly produce the result you wanted.

Leadership 25. Lead Me, Please! ⌘ page 45

It's so easy to be a follower, even when there are opportunities to be a leader.

Leadership 26. Second Life ⌘ page 45

Let's apply Dwight's philosophy to people we'd otherwise label "broken."

Leadership 27. Pressing Matters ⌘ page 46

For your next project, work out the pressing details but be prepared for the unintended consequences.

Leadership 28. Itching to Succeed ⌘ page 46

Make it easy for people to succeed. Set up the environment so they can take control of the outcome of their efforts.

Leadership 29. Management Training ⌘ page 47

To be successful, anticipate, watch what's coming next, and don't worry about the past.

Leadership 30. Better Decisions ⌘ page 47

Surround yourself with healthy, wise choices – and a plate you can handle.

Cultural Notes and Lexical Challenges

⌘ Life ⌘

Life 1. Driving with Devon ⌘ page 1
Cultural Note

Boston is one of the oldest cities in the United States. Over the past 380 years, it has evolved from unpaved streets suitable for foot and horse traffic to modern car, truck, train, and bus transportation. Traffic patterns have been changed without a comprehensive plan. As a result, the many one-way and restricted streets make navigation of the city confusing for outsiders.

Lexical Challenges

- autism • to dread • to irritate • to recite • a copilot

Life 2. The Need to Talk ⌘ page 1
Lexical Challenges

- to look forward to • distressing • the doldrums • bleak
- blaring • emphatically

Life 3. Culture Norms ⌘ page 3
Lexical Challenges

- congested • dodging

Life 4. How Big is Home? ⌘ page 2
Cultural Note

An interstate is a high-speed highway, part of the national highway system.

Lexical Challenges

- a license plate • a diner

Life 5. Stay Inside the Lines ⌘ page 3
Lexical Challenges

- an endorsement

Life 6. The Passing Lane ⌘ page 3
Cultural Note

Passing safely – Many highways through the countryside have only one lane of traffic traveling in each direction. Because of frequent curves and hills, some roadways do not have many safe places to pass slower traffic. In these instances, an additional traffic lane might be built alongside the right lane going up a hill. Slower-moving vehicles are required to use the far right lane so that those who wish to pass can use the middle lane without crossing into oncoming traffic.

Lexical Challenges

• lumbering • bumper to bumper • mph

Life 7. Spreading the Word ⌘ page 4
Lexical Challenges

• an amusement park • a rollercoaster • brain numb
• to cut one's losses • to speculate

Life 8. Enough Time ⌘ page 4
Lexical Challenges

• adequate • allotted • to accomplish • sternly • harsh

Life 9. Being Present ⌘ page 5
Lexical Challenges

• a buddy • a Buddhist • meditation • an extension
• contemplative • to saunter • goggles

Life 10. Instant Friendships ⌘ page 5
Cultural Note

Beetle and Subaru – A beetle or "bug" is a small car with a distinctive rounded shape manufactured by the Volkswagen Corporation of Germany. Beetles have been common in the United States since the late 1950's. A Subaru is a four-wheel-drive automobile manufactured by the Subaru Corporation of Japan. The Subaru is a very common car in the Northeastern United States because of its reliability on slippery winter roads.

Lexical Challenges

- zooming • to grab • slimmest thread

Life 11. Always in Crisis ⌘ page 6
Lexical Challenges

- case manager • a client • to dash • juggling • a crisis

Life 12. Room to Wiggle ⌘ page 6
Lexical Challenges

- wiggle room • to flip • plumbing • guts

Life 13. Reboot ⌘ page 7
Lexical Challenges

- to reboot • on the fritz • to sync • to pull the plug
- a feedback loop

Life 14. Preoccupation ⌘ page 7
Lexical Challenges

- a wheelchair • to grasp • to retrieve

Life 15. A Public Statement ⌘ page 8
Cultural Note

Just married car decorations – When a couple is married, they drive from the ceremony or from the reception to begin their honeymoon in a car that has been decorated by their friends. People write messages, such as "Just Married," in non-permanent shaving cream or on cardboard signs taped to the car. They may also tie strings of empty cans to the back bumper intended to make noise as the couple drives away.

Lexical Challenges

- dented • rust • stenciled • nuptial • to marvel
- deliberately • resale value • lovesick • perpetual

Life 16. The Trivial Things ⌘ page 8
Cultural Note

A deck is a location for recreation outside and usually attached to a house. It consists of a wooden platform on low posts or other simple foundation. It may have a railing to prevent falls and it may have a roof. The floor is made of boards or planks laid parallel to one another but with a gap of a few centimeters between them.

Lexical Challenges

- to reprimand • over the top

Life 17. Tired of Retirement ⌘ page 9
Lexical Challenges

- a reputation • to thrive • literally • to lose one's mind
- listless • dementia • vibrant

Life 18. Personal Issues ⌘ page 9
Lexical Challenges

- sheepishly • evidently • in spite of • reassurances
- chagrined

Life 25. Imagine! ⌘ page 13
Cultural Note

Martha's Vineyard – Martha's Vineyard is an island in the Atlantic Ocean off the coast of Massachusetts. Its location midway between New York City and Boston, along with its relatively undeveloped beaches, makes it a popular though expensive vacation destination.

Lexical Challenges

- fond of • well-being • to hesitate • a gull • to heal
- a lasting impact • surf

Life 26. Your Center ⌘ page 13
Cultural Note

Basque and fronton – The Basque people have inhabited the mountainous region overlapping the border between France and Spain since before recorded history. Their language and culture are distinct from the Latin and Roman-based cultures of the surrounding area. Fronton is a game for two to four players who hit a small ball, usually with their bare hands. The ball is hit toward a wall at the front of the court and may bounce off a perpendicular side wall before being returned.

Lexical Challenges

- foremost

Life 27. Writer's Block ⌘ page 14
Lexical Challenges

- slush • to shovel • to grumble • crisp • a state of flow

Life 28. Focus of Attention ⌘ page 14
Lexical Challenges

- a neon sign • a vendor • to captivate • to ignore

Life 29. Wants and Needs ⌘ page 15
Cultural Note

St. Patrick's Day – St. Patrick was a 5th-century Catholic missionary and bishop who is revered as the patron saint of Ireland. March 17, the date of his death, is celebrated in many countries. In the United States, the date is celebrated by many who are not religious as a festival about Ireland and everything Irish.

Lexical Challenges

• an announcement • to snatch

Life 30. Perspective ⌘ page 15
Lexical Challenges

• particular • inquisitiveness • the novel • the norm

Life 31. Threats ⌘ page 16
Cultural Note

Town Meeting/ambulance service – Once a year, many communities in New England have a town meeting to conduct business such as approval of budgets for the school, road maintenance, the fire department, and the town administrative office. Any resident of the town who is of legal age may speak and vote at the meeting. Ambulance service refers to a private organization which provides emergency medical treatment and transportation to a hospital if needed. An ambulance service company will negotiate and contract to provide service to a town or region. Members of a town may vote to approve such a contract at a town meeting.

Lexical Challenges

• representative • to debate • furiously • threatened

Life 32. Doing the Dishes ⌘ page 16
Lexical Challenges

• to get a handle on • to hide

⌘ Learning ⌘

Learning 1. Turn Right to Go Left ⌘ page 17
Lexical Challenges

- to coincide • to flow • to switch • original intent

Learning 2. Wasting Work Time ⌘ page 17
Lexical Challenges

- to waste • social capital

Learning 3. Looking and Finding ⌘ page 18
Cultural Note

Bird watching – Bird watching is a pastime activity in which people seek to find and identify various species of birds in the wild. Bird watchers may use binoculars and reference books. They may also keep a record of the species they have identified, their location, and the date they found them.

Lexical Challenges

- a bird watcher • a raptor • a hawk • an owl • stealthy
- nocturnal • broad daylight

Learning 4. Limits ⌘ page 18
Lexical Challenges

- a dip • satin

Learning 5. Teaching a Lesson ⌘ page 19
Cultural Note

Home Economics – Home Economics is a course of study in many American high schools which focuses on maintaining a house and home. It can include food preparation and nutrition, sewing, and small electrical, carpentry, and plumbing repairs as well as child development and managing money.

Lexical Challenges

- Home Economics • to beat • to click • to scold

Learning 6. Too Much Talk! ⌘ page 19
Lexical Challenges

- heart-to-heart • reflections • pubescent • glazed eyes
- slouched • tuned out

Learning 7. Who Knew? ⌘ page 20
Lexical Challenges

- a pacifier • a junkie • daycare • to induce
- to kick the habit • carcinogenic • cold turkey

Learning 8. The Wrong Notes ⌘ page 20
Lexical Challenges

- pursuit • preoccupation • a saxophone solo • a spirited rendition

Learning 9. 100,000 Teachers ⌘ page 21
Lexical Challenges

- traumatic • tailoring • a replacement

Learning 10. Overdue and Unprepared ⌘ page 21
Cultural Note

State inspection – Vehicles in every state must be inspected annually to insure they are safe and reliable. The inspection must be done by a qualified mechanic; a label is attached to the car, usually on the front windshield, indicating the date of the latest inspection.

Lexical Challenges

- overdue • an annual safety inspection • insurance papers
- to keep me on my toes

Learning 11. On Mobility ⌘ page 22
Cultural Note

Rural Church – A rural church is a building that houses a religious community or congregation. It may be in the countryside or in a small village, but it does not have a physical connection to a large city. Because it is in a less populous area, it may not have very many members or very large financial resources.

Lexical Challenges

- rollers • a strawberry supper • a Christmas bazaar
- everything but the kitchen sink • a foundation
- to accommodate

Learning 12. On a Roll ⌘ page 22
Lexical Challenges

- a counter • handy • to dispense • a nuisance

Learning 13. A Crumby Day ⌘ page 23
Lexical Challenges

- out of sorts • crumby • an earful • lousy

Learning 14. A Perfect Smile ⌘ page 23
Lexical Challenges

- fluoride treatment • symmetry • underlying
- an assumption • ethnicity

Learning 15. A Father's Choice ⌘ page 24
Lexical Challenges

- to pick out • flair • skinny • swishy • to reject
- to bother

Learning 16. Sugar Coating ⌘ page 24
Lexical Challenges

- a cinnamon roll • slathered • frosting • a substance
- to resemble • a woolen mitten • to store • calories
- first rate

Learning 17. Less is More ⌘ page 25
Cultural Note

Interactive learning – Interactive learning is education that combines knowledge and practice. Students are presented with information and given opportunities to improve skills that use that information. It emphasizes critical analysis of information, testing of ideas, feedback from teachers and other students, and application of learning outside of the classroom. It is often considered the opposite of lecture-style learning, in which students listen passively to an expert who tells them information.

Lexical Challenges

- a facilitator • interactive learning strategies
- a blaring electronic alarm • weird • a participant

Learning 18. In Sight ⌘ page 25
Lexical Challenges

- alternative resources • coping strategies • reflective
- to concentrate • to reinforce

Learning 19. Deliver the Message ⌘ page 26
Lexical Challenges

- to encounter • a civil rights lawyer • vulnerable
- to highlight

Learning 20. First Amendment ⌘ page 26
Cultural Note

First Amendment/Bumper sticker – The First Amendment to the Constitution of the United States guarantees the right of free speech, the right to meet as a group for peaceful purposes, the right to receive compensation for damages the government has caused, and the right to freely exercise one's religious beliefs, and prohibits the establishment of a state religion. A bumper sticker is a small sign, usually about 30 cm by 10 cm, attached to the back of a car. Most often, messages are political, humorous, or in support of a sport-team.

Lexical Challenges

- a bumper sticker • to reveal • contemplative • caustic
- to tailgate • sake • to signify • a sound bite
- a catchy phrase • to accelerate • to formulate

Learning 21. An Empty Desk ⌘ page 27
Lexical Challenges

- a multi-tasker • a deadline • a grant • to rearrange
- to stack • to dust • funded

Learning 22. Mud Season ⌘ page 27
Cultural Note

Mud Season – In regions with heavy snowfall, there is a time in early spring when snow and ice are melting rapidly. There can be a few weeks when the surface snow is melting but the soil several centimeters below ground level is still frozen. When this happens, the melting snow cannot be absorbed into the ground. As a result, the top layer of soil is very soft and muddy. If this occurs on an unpaved road, cars can sink into the softened roadway and get stuck.

Lexical Challenges

- muddy • garbage • a dumpster • to inch • unpaved
- sloppy tracks • muck • to grab • to steer
- to scrape bottom • to speed off • a rut

Learning 23. Dead and Alive ⌘ page 28
Cultural Note

Maple syrup – Maple syrup is a sweetener made from the sap of the maple tree, a deciduous hardwood that grows in the northeast United States and eastern Canada. In early spring, the sap flows up from the roots where it was stored during winter so that the tree can generate new leaves. When a small hole is drilled in the side of the tree and a metal tube is inserted, the sap can be collected and boiled to evaporate the water it contains. The resulting liquid is maple syrup, used on pancakes and in cooking and baking.

Lexical Challenges

- a grove • sugar maples • a stump • soaking wet
- a puddle • sap • raw material • maple syrup
- loggers

Learning 24. High Expectations ⌘ page 28
Lexical Challenges

- to decipher • frustrated • simultaneously
- a native speaker

Learning 25. Ask Stupid Questions ⌘ page 29
Lexical Challenges

- a light switch • a query • an electric shock • ignorant

Learning 26. Try Again ⌘ page 29
Lexical Challenges

- a tightrope walker • a spectacular stunt • jaded
- entangled • to erupt • applause

Learning 27. Potential ⌘ page 30
Lexical Challenges

- journalism • a grant writer • to materialize • would-be
- executive director material • self-concept

Learning 28. Oops? ⌘ page 30
Cultural Note

Vanity Plates – Every car in the United States must have a metal identification tag, or license plate, issued by the state where the owner lives, on the back bumper. Some states allow car owners to customize the lettering on their license plate for an additional fee. People use these special plates to say something about themselves, but because there is only room for six or seven characters, it can be difficult to figure out the message that is being stated.

Lexical Challenges

- error free • remorse • to bulldoze • a mystic

Learning 29. Real Lessons ⌘ page 31
Lexical Challenges

- to volunteer • disadvantaged • crushed

Learning 30. Missed Messages ⌘ page 31
Lexical Challenges

- to board • a flight • blaring • a PA system • hazardous
- a checkpoint • to strip • offending • to drown out
- a gate change

Learning 31. The Slow Learner ⌘ page 32
Cultural Note

Screened porch – Many homes have a low platform outside the house to access the front or back door. Sometimes this platform is large enough for several chairs and a small table, providing a place to enjoy the cool air in summertime. It may be enclosed with a metal or cloth mesh screen which allows light and airflow with protection from mosquitos and flies.

Lexical Challenges

- sweltering • relief • a screened porch • enormous
- a housefly • to bounce • charitable • to bash into
- a right angle

Learning 32. Happiness ⌘ page 32
Lexical Challenges

- caretaker • siblings • hardships • pessimisitic

⌘ Leadership ⌘

Leadership 1. Creating Change ⌘ page 33
Lexical Challenges

- a pang of hunger • a quick fix • a fistful
- munching away • to diminish

Leadership 2. What's Your Contribution? ⌘ page 33
Lexical Challenges

- to witness • demeanor • droll • sarcastic • grumbling
- to get something out of something

Leadership 3. Empowerment ⌘ page 34
Cultural Note

Retreats – A retreat is a special meeting designed for office staff to make plans and decisions or to improve work relationships and develop as professionals. A retreat is usually held away from the worksite and led by an outside consultant. Retreats can last from one half day to as long as three days.

Lexical Challenges

- a coach • a supervisor • to strive • potential • acutely
- to discriminate • to confide • fancy

Leadership 4. Taking a Stand on Meetings ⌘ page 34
Lexical Challenges

- to assume • to accomplish • to spread the table

Leadership 5. Climbing Toward Goals ⌘ page 35
Lexical Challenges

- frequently • fitness hikers • panoramic • a summit
- a vista • solitude

Leadership 6. The Best Holiday ⌘ page 35
  Cultural Note

  'Twas the day after Christmas. "'Twas" is a contraction of "it was," a term more common in older styles of English. "'Twas the day after Christmas" is a reference to the first line of a famous poem, "A Visit from St. Nicholas," by Clement Clarke Moore. The poem begins, "'Twas the night before Christmas, when all thro' the house / Not a creature was stirring, not even a mouse." It goes on to describe Santa Claus flying through the air, entering the house, and delivering presents.

  Lexical Challenges

  • unfortunately • one's own devices

Leadership 7. Seeing the Big Picture ⌘ page 36
  Lexical Challenges

  • a metro area • fortunately • equipped
  • GPS navigation system • a handy device • rush hour
  • a readout • a prompt • counterintuitive
  • disconcerting

Leadership 8. Hot? Cold? ⌘ page 36
  Lexical Challenges

  • a lap swimmer • a stressor • acclimated

Leadership 9. Choose Chaos ⌘ page 37
  Lexical Challenges

  • chaos • potentialities • a boundary • randomness
  • an outcome • unpredictable

Leadership 10. Who's to Blame? ⌘ page 37
  Lexical Challenges

  • pollution • a culprit • a coal-fired power plant
  • to contend with

Leadership 11. Being the Crowd ⌘ page 38
Lexical Challenges

- to overhear • grumbling • a buddy • irony

Leadership 12. Trash or Treasure ⌘ page 38
Lexical Challenges

- junk • a label • to accumulate • bent • charred
- a craft project

Leadership 13. Built to Last ⌘ page 39
Cultural Note

Incan, Machu Picchu, SUV – The Incans were an indigenous people of South America who had the largest empire in the Western Hemisphere before Europeans arrived. Their civilization was eventually conquered by the Spanish in 1572. Machu Picchu was an Incan city probably built for the emperor. It is situated on a conical mountain top in the Andean Mountains of Peru. SUV is an abbreviation for Sport Utility Vehicle, a type of automobile that is very large, with four-wheel drive and the capability to travel over difficult roads and through deep snow or sand.

Lexical Challenges

- to last • ruins • mortar • to fashion • withstood
- an earthquake • to crumble

Leadership 14. Open for Business? ⌘ page 39
Cultural Note

Booth – A booth is a type of seating arrangement in casual restaurants. The narrow end of a table is fixed to the wall. Each of the long sides of the table is furnished with an upholstered bench that can seat two to three people on each side. People enter the booth by sliding onto the bench at the open end. Booths are popular because they feel more intimate for a small group, and because of the many nostalgic references to them in American movies.

Lexical Challenges

- to savor • startled • deserted

Leadership 15. The Accidental Leader ⌘ page 40
Lexical Challenges

- a corridor • coincidental • to tease • to quip

Leadership 16. Motion Sickness ⌘ page 40
Lexical Challenges

- fall foliage • poetic • picturesque • to navigate
- accustomed to • a green tinge • a complexion

Leadership 17. Simply Exact ⌘ page 41
Lexical Challenges

- precise • an essay • to occur • clarification • to outline
- an implication • clarity • a fog of confusion • obscured

Leadership 18. Great Groups ⌘ page 41
Cultural Note

Calls at square dances – A square dance is a dance in which four couples face each other, with each couple forming one side of a square. There can be many squares of dancers but they only dance in squares of eight. The caller is a leader who provides directions and dance steps for the moves dancers will make.

Lexical Challenges

- a choral group • a mean accordion • fostering teamwork
- in charge • a novice • to summarize • to harmonize
- uniquely

Leadership 19. Turning and Changing ⌘ page 42
Lexical Challenges

- balancing • awkward • to lean

Leadership 20. Motivation That's Habit Forming ⌘ page 42
Lexical Challenges

- eventually • a household cleaner • a warning label
- prominent • obvious • to be cool • social • belonging

Leadership 21. Making Changes ⌘ page 43
Lexical Challenges

- to facilitate • a participant • ensuing chaos • to conspire
- a buddy • intact

Leadership 22. No, Gracias ⌘ page 43
Lexical Challenges

- to burst • to evaluate • to digest

Leadership 23. All Together ⌘ page 44
Lexical Challenges

- spirited conversation • to burst into song • boisterous
- to rattle

Leadership 24. Change Recipe ⌘ page 44
Cultural Note

Thanksgiving – Thanksgiving is a holiday celebrated on the last Thursday in November in the U.S. and on the second Monday of October in Canada. In the U.S., the holiday commemorates the first year of survival of the Pilgrims when they were new immigrants to North America. After a difficult winter and trouble adjusting to a new environment, the early settlers received help from the Native Americans, who taught them new methods of planting, harvesting, and fishing. The Pilgrims set aside a time to feast, celebrate, and give thanks. Today, families gather and prepare a large banquet to celebrate Thanksgiving.

Lexical Challenges

- homemade • a recipe • a jelly jar • to jiggle
- to vibrate • to wobble • to agitate • to give up
- persistence • a lump • magically

Leadership 25, Lead Me, Please! ⌘ page 45
Cultural Note

Aerobics club – Aerobics is a type of exercise that seeks to increase the heart rate while maximizing oxygen intake. The goal is to have one's heart work at 60% to 80% of its capacity. Aerobic exercises include walking, jogging, running, cycling, and swimming. An aerobics club is an exercise center where groups of people exercise in unison following the directions of a leader or teacher. The leader directs them in a variety of moves and steps to keep their hearts working at the desired rate.

Lexical Challenges

- obvious • Senior Aerobics Club • to chat • a routine
- bossy

Leadership 26. Second Life ⌘ page 45
Lexical Challenges

- a tattered dish towel • threadbare • to dismiss
- a hopeless eccentric • undying • an expectation

Leadership 27. Pressing Matters ⌘ page 46
Lexical Challenges

- pressing • an agenda • refreshments • an outcome
- critical • to factor • implications • a permanent crease

Leadership 28. Itching to Succeed ⌘ page 46
Lexical Challenges

- prickling • a collar • a barber • a smock • a dusting
- a whisk • clippings

Leadership 29. Management Training ⌘ page 47
Lexical Challenges

- to juggle • a scarf • to toss • to descend

Leadership 30. Better Decisions ⌘ page 47
Lexical Challenges

- a muffin • loaded down

Write Your Own Lesson

and Conclusion

Other books from Pro Lingua

AT THE HIGH-INTERMEDIATE AND ADVANCED LEVELS

Books by David and Peggy Kehe

❖ **Cultural Differences** — David and Peggy Kehe's newest book is a content-based college/university preparation course introducing and giving practice in using a wide range of academic skills. It is of value to English language learners and native speakers who are or will be living in a culturally diverse environment.

The content is focused on a neglected area of language-culture studies: the confusion, misunderstandings, misconceptions, and sometimes even hostilities that can occur when learners don't really understand each other's langue and culture.

Cultural Differences is actually two books, the **Basic Text** and the *photocopyable* **Supplementary Activities**. The Basic Text can be used alone. Using the two books together provides a more challenging program. The supplementary materials involve the learner in a deeper exploration of how and why people from collectivist and individualist cultures differ.

❖ **Discussion Strategies** — Carefully structured pair and small-group work at the high-intermediate level. Excellent preparation for students who will participate in academic or professional work that requires effective participation in discussion and seminars.

❖ **The Grammar Review Book** — This easy-to-use book is designed for anyone who has learned English by ear and who needs to write grammatically. The students learn to recognize and correct common, fossilized errors through a carefully sequenced series of exercises.

❖ **Writing Strategies** — There are two volumes in this student-centered essay-writing course. Each introduces four types of essay, in four rhetorical modes, following a writing-editing process, a careful sequence of steps from preparing the first draft to writing the final essay. The four modes in Book One at the high-intermediate level are Description, Narration, Exposition, and Comparison and Contrast. The modes in Book Two at the Advanced level are Process, Cause and Effect, Extended Definition, and Argumentation. The essay writing is augmented by two supplementary activities in the second and third sections of each book.

Fluency Writing. In pairs and triads, the students exchange information on a contemporary topic. They finish the activity by summarizing in writing what they have discussed.

Grammar Problems and Terminology. In this section, the students review those pesky grammar problems that always show up in the process of putting thoughts into grammatically accurate sentences. These are recommended if needed at specific points in the essay-writing process.

Also **Teaching in the United States** *for International Educators* by Dr. Julie Damron